Douglas, Me & James

poems by

Vin Whitman

Finishing Line Press
Georgetown, Kentucky

Douglas, Me & James

*For my friends at the Midwest Cafe, where this book was written
Also for Douglas, James, and Pixel*

Publisher: Leah Huete de Maines
Editor: Christen Kincaid
Cover Art: Vin Whitman
Author Photo: Tony Egler
Cover Design: Elizabeth Maines McCleavy

Order online: www.finishinglinepress.com
also available on amazon.com

Author inquiries and mail orders:
Finishing Line Press
PO Box 1626
Georgetown, Kentucky 40324
USA

Contents

Part One: Douglas

Douglas 1
Me? Me?! 3
Scullery 4
Reverse Image Search 5
7 of Swords 6
In Person 7
Recalling 9
Gallery 10

Part Two: Me

Intimately Clawing the Rungs 11
Hands Free 12
My Initial Reaction 13
Slow Processor 14
Minuet for Douglas 15
Minuet for James 16
Invisible Now 17
Supreme Speculation 18

Part Three: James

I Got Sick; You Got Bored 19
Seethe Through 20
Deep Ploy 22
New Horror 23
July 21 24
Deep Vices 25
Apple Corpse 26
Just Stop 27
Clean, But 28
Blue Horror 29
James 1 30
What To Make of Akathisia Thru a Blue Lens 32
James 2 33

PART ONE: DOUGLAS

_____

_____

DOUGLAS

Because I'm sick with boredom
Of poems about food & children

Endless noticing
Of bees, flowers, oceans,

I wanted to tell the story of you,
Douglas,
And me,
And our decade of digital freeze tag

It wasn't flirting
Or romance
But was it harassment?
Trespassing?
Any violation that could be prosecuted?

You sent me a friend request
In the autumn of 2009

I didn't know you
So I ignored it

In 2009 friends were friends
And fuzzy-named strangers were easily forgotten

One late, late night
You called in to the radio station

Where I did a show w/ a sidekick
Who loved to stand on the shoulders of giants

You raved about our show,
And my song choices in particular

My co-host raved
About your shoulders & said

If I were wise
I'd add you to my collection of close allies

I accepted his counsel
And your request was granted

Me? ME?!

I didn't see what was so great about you

You lifted lots of memes
From 4chan or Reddit

You begged for donations (for a cause
You wouldn't even divulge)

You offered me no writing opportunities,
Which my co-host promised were yours

To hand out.
You flew below my radar until April 2010

When you posted the most misogynist meme
I'd ever seen

I responded with a friendly dose of disapproval.
You liked that.

SCULLERY

We'd already found new ways to torment
Each other in the infant stages
Of social media

There were no ads on the walls
There were no community standards
The algorithm lay in its crib

Swaddled & suckling
Waiting for its bones to fuse
Waiting for a crisp diaper & a bowl of oats

You already had better ideas
I was just happy to be "part of the conversation"

All my life…
My timid voice…
My crowd-sourced reticence…

My identity hidden
Under a skin that lay pathologically pretty

My fingers ached to tell a truth
Infused with all my years of observation

You wanted money & attention
I wanted to blow the tops of peoples' skulls back open

REVERSE IMAGE SEARCH

It was a dawn slowly drying
A digital watercolor dripping into view

One day I noticed
How much we had in common

Every meme you'd cleverly found—
The master forager—

Seemed to pertain to something I too
Had alluded to

In writing,
In passing thru Farmville
On my way to a friendlier place,

Something I had thought
To observe out loud &

There you were
Responding with borrowed humor
Clapping back w/ protracted hands

Oh your other 4,999 friends were delighted!

Where did you find such gems?

You wouldn't give an ounce
Not an inch of information

I stopped wondering about your shoulders
And started searching for your face…

7 of SWORDS

In the land of infinite selfies
In the realm of scanned remember-whens

You were nowhere to be found

You hoarded 5,000 penniless friends &
Stayed invisible behind a daily switcheroo

Of biting memes

Unsound in their cynicism, but you?
Untouchable?
Ugly enough to kill an army of Gorgons?
Under witness protection?

For some reason you did not
Want to show up

And in those early days, before the fakes,
I felt this was very unfair

You were cheating at Facebook &
I decided I really didn't like it

IN PERSON

Still there were times you made me laugh
W/ your humor customized

To reflect like chrome
My every thought, feeling

As freshly shaven as a blown
Dandelion & your fuzz, your haze

Remained the face
You wouldn't show to the world

I finally met you in person
Oct 9, 2010

Everyone loved you! How they greeted you
W/ enthusiasm and…was it respect?

What did they see in you?
I saw a plain man in a plaid shirt

Pretty short. Your face indeed fuzzy,
A mess really, unshaven moss rock

Rolling toward me as I bent over
Painting a sign for the grand opening

Of the new station.
You hovered above me

All 5'6" shadow of your mossiness.
My radio friend,

Painting w/ me,
Introduced you formally

Though I'd already put 2 &
2 together.

You had no guilt in your
Conscience yet

You hovered &
With your utmost bossiness

Addressed me,
"You better watch out."

I kept painting quietly.

"What? Nothing?"
You waited for something.

Down you stared.
I pressed my tank top closer to my chest.

You mumbled and walked away.
I went to find the broken bottle of glitter.

RECALLING

I'm writing this 12 years in the future &
What I remember

Is ignoring you with all my might
While you semaphored urgently, sophomorically

Resorting to hits below the belt
Reaching for my pubes w/ your mental pincers

& finding just a bald spot. I wouldn't give.

Not an inch. Not a smile.
Not a little blue thumb.

But I remained
                    Curious
                    Cautious
                    Skeptical
        Friends w/ you

GALLERY

You finally lured your followers
To speak the words

You knew would
Dump my higher ground in the gutter

"Transsexuals are disgusting"
   (I'm paraphrasing)

But you said it
Through the innocent megaphones of bystanders &

You smeared Peanuts one by one,
Giving them all new genders

I recognized Peppermint Pat
Playing me in your charade

One of your "friends" was PUKING

SO MUCH HATE
You led them to express so freely

I had to formulate a response,
A defense of my kind. So I did

I responded, I defended
Myself against puking & hatred

But the stalemate was done.
I was Peppermint Pat from there on.

On May 28, 2014
I blocked you (& several others)
In pursuit of my own peace

[instead a year of akathisia, a side effect
That affected me in worse ways than you ever could]

PART TWO: ME

_____

_____

INTIMATELY CLAWING THE RUNGS

I knew how you & your 5,000 friends
Felt about the way
I was about to turn the Universe
On its edge

Cartwheeling into an Aeon unknown
So far from the hamster wheel galaxy
You had dominated
For centuries

You'd lost your mother
Before any other treasure

Your father held you & you grew

                              Feet,
                    A beard,
            An ego w/ oxen shoulders

You were an elder (spin) doctor

Better than me, for sure

So…what on Earth did you need?

HANDS FREE

Honestly I'd wiped you
From all the screens & lenses in my life.

All of them,
Including that untouchable, invisible,
Archetypal, prototypical

Lens that looks in.

Sure in dark moments
I'd remember you were there &
What you'd done

But mostly my screens were lit
By devilish pixels

My lenses smudged by
Money shots

Mostly my time was spent
Floating weightless on all the tears
I'd cried the year before

The salt now a savior
Instead of an anchor

MY INITIAL REACTION

It was on the day
Of my legal name change

I realized your salty pupils were still upon me

Back when Facebook would notify us
That someone we knew commented
On someone else we knew (or didn't)

You appeared as commentee
On a mutual screen
(you were blocked on mine, remember)

One of my friend's friends
Thought it was super-awesome-nifty-thumbs-up-likable
That you'd changed your profile pic
To a caravan of Volkswagen beetles
Crawling over the crooked horizon

My initial reaction was a shrug
It looked like you'd moved along
To your own new horizon

Then I realized
My initial reaction was wrong

SLOW PROCESSOR

The author of this narrative
Beseeches you to check & recheck the cover,

Your logarithmic
Processor of words & dates,

To recognize Time as the force
That nudges us off-stage

Over the horizon of applause

Aloft I tried to stay
On the raw nerves
That had strung me to the atmosphere since 1970

You would be there
No matter what I did
Like the wind & sun &
The screeching hum
Of voluntary surveillance
Created in our attempt to access porn

My name is VW & I am not your free ride

MINUET FOR DOUGLAS

How?
Sprung from lifeless loins.

What?
A smiling Leo sun.

Who?
Your father was raised by a constellation of kings.

Why?
The telephone died. The lines roared. Together they hung
themselves.

When?
The beat era.

Where?
An American wilderness, lion-free.

MINUET FOR JAMES

For a minute you sing the consonants
Instead of the vowels &
That's impossible

But not for you

Your song born of brain chemistry
Far exceeding the hype of any reuptake inhibitor

Swells without time
Your signature is illegible
Your heart incorruptible

****

Elevated
On your brain-song
I wander in on you & add black lines &
Circles,

Open & closed,
Sent from so many places on the staff

From the clubs of Indianapolis,
To the rocks of Utah & the hills
Of Hollywood

I brought you down step by step,
Drop by drop
Note by note

INVISIBLE NOW

Silence is to the ears
As darkness is to the eyes
But the touch of a beetle is rough
Not ticklish &

Somewhere the wires crossed
Now I can't tell silence
From a bug's toe,

Antennae from a candle lit bistro

Somewhere between axis & atlas
The wires tore like tendons &
Left a draft where sparks do their

Jumping Jacks

Now brain activity—
Not so much thoughts but moods,
Impulses, involuntary reactions—

That activity is detectable
By eyes & ears & touch
By candle's light & cockroach sole

The wires crossed & I'm not sure
I'm still computing

SUPREME SPECULATION

Maybe you aren't the bored upstart,
                                    the attention whore

Maybe you wanted to scare me,
                    Make me feel my inferiority
                                So acutely

I'd crumple at your electric toes
            Keys, taps, I'd rapture

From my unclean skin

As your strokes of loneliness
Posed as power,
                    Truth,
                Rationale

But
Maybe you ARE the bored attention-whore upstart
                            Sophomore lawnmower

Maybe you're really, really scared
                Of my divine inferiority

PART THREE: JAMES

I GOT SICK; YOU GOT BORED

Some great swarm of sick-flies
Came on the breeze

In true viral fashion
They wore incurable combat boots

Masked the airwaves &
Sent canned programming out

To the isolated
Ears/mouths/noses in wait

An audience starved of performance
Arts   music
Business   company

& boredom infected all the boring people

While the thinkers/inventors/entrepreneurs
Thrived like playful dolphins

I got sick
But not with the swarm
You got bored &
Slid onto my screen again

SEETHE THROUGH

When I saw your bored sickness
ONCE AGAIN

Ten years was enough
I removed my block
I named you the Godfather of all Trolls
Right there in the comments

Your followers accused me
Of skipping my meds

But that's not what it was. I kept my eyes & ears
Clean & quiet & open &
Waited

*****

Now you could see me &
I could see you

And it didn't take long before
The pattern emerged

Once again YOU
Stitching extra tentacles

To my immersive octopus
As I propelled

From thought to thought
    Garden to garden
   Post office to psychiatrist's office

Never standing on anyone's shoulders
But seeing right thru
   Solid objects
Into the next revelation

My vision would be
Paralyzed
By the modern crystal ball

Bounced from the big tech clubs
That allowed bored people like you

To bleed thru velvet ropes
Laugh glass ceilings into micro-chips

& access mundane snapshots
Of now, not whenever

DEEP PLOY

When I named you Godfather Troll
In the public eye

The game was on, apparently

Some undersea bullfight
Where the matadors were men
But their prey was soft & squishy

Without horns or hooves
With only ink as defense

You depleted my implements

My softness, squishiness, inkiness
Welled up at every swash,
                    grope, splash

In the quiet moments
After each onslaught,
I would survey the damage

Where were the corpses to be lain?
Why did you know things
You could only know

If you were opening my skull,
Breaking my door down,
Unlocking my windows w/ passwords you'd stolen?

You, no genius or hacker,
Had soldiers deployed

I was alone against your army

NEW HORROR

When you realize
Someone's watching you

A cold wind blows through your veins

You stand there like a crazy-straw

Leaking solid particles of yourself

All your blood blown against
                        Some wall faraway

All your curated confidence demolished

For what other confidence do you have?
            Is there another kind
            Deep inside you
That subconsciously decides you are worthy
                        Of peace,
                        Privacy,
                        Justice?

Or are you alone with 7 swords
Hacking into your bathroom routine,
                        Your porn stash,
                        Your dopamine centers?

[Did you see me fall to the tile, sobbing
Full tubs of anguish everyday & trying to languish
In that sudden hemorrhage of happiness?]

JULY 21

On July 21, 2020 I told you, James, to leave
Your phone inside & come with me
Out to the porch

I told you all about Douglas
What had been happening for 10 years

& how it had somehow breached
New borders

That in fact, there were no borders

There were no boundaries, no blinders,
No curtains, no clothes
No mute button
No fun filters
No opt-out options

We'd been reduced to somebody's SIMS
& they wore our actual skins

It's not possible, you said.
Our devices are infallible.

DEEP VICES

But what about the human component,
I asked. The technology isn't doing this,
A person is.

Shrugs. Bafflement. Disbelief.

Can you just look at his posts & tell me what you think?

Shrugs. Annoyance. Disbelief.

I mean, some of it is aimed at you...

Shrugs. Denial. Disbelief.

We scrolled thru the incriminating memes;
(Was he incriminating himself, or indicting me?)

One thing we agreed upon—it all bore
A striking resemblance

To the discord of our inner sanctum

And still the shrugs
Still the pause
Still the faith in almighty technology

APPLE CORPSE

Because you refused to even consider it,
I got to consider it a lot (for both of us)

& it weighed on me like a naked corpse
'til I became the naked corpse

Weighing my own sanity,
                    My own keen observation,
                    My own sober judgement
Against the magic of artificial intellect

And leaving the morgue behind,
I still believed in me.

The corpse was real. The corpse was near.
The corpse was making sounds & smells
That swallowed the air & foul'd the rooms.

It wasn't enough
I'd collected scrolls of evidence—

Look! Didn't we just say this to each other
                    yesterday?
Isn't this where we ate last night?
How did he know we bought a yellow chair?
The words I spoke to my brother on the phone,
        spat back in some hastily drawn cartoon?
How'd he duplicate this doodle
            From my [paper] notebook?

Is this really just coincidence?

You swallowed the Artificial Benevolence
        of our computer, tv, iPad screens

JUST STOP

"If you're interrogating me,
We should interrogate the technology"

This was your philosophy. So I agreed
Yes, let's interrogate each device

We waited in line, masked, at veriZon

While one angry man refused
To cover his face & threatened violence

In real life.

We waited out the spectacle
& finally our artifice-detective
Gave us a thorough read

No embedded code
No insecure log-ins
No techno-lice

"There", you said.
"Now you can stop worrying about this."

CLEAN, BUT

We took our devices
To one more place,
The Apple Store

The detective there said everything
Was spotless,
Clean as a clergyman's whistle,
Unpirated,
Unhacked,
So fucking secure, so goddamned airtight,
A true piece of intelligent, benevolent,
                                  Aristocratic machinery!

But…said the detective…
               I would put a piece of tape
                    Over the camera

BLUE HORROR

So I tore a piece of blue masking tape
Off a roll that cost $3.59

& I placed it over the super hi-def
Uber-pixelated color-saturated
$2K camera lens

I walked outside, onto my porch &
Spent the rest of the sweltering FL summer there,

Leaving all my expensive devices
Alone in an empty room

Believing you'd get bored
If you couldn't watch me cry, or
Hear me pee

I read books, wrote poetry, turned
My radio up so loud the leaf-blowers cringed

The next time I dared to check on you,
Your profile pic was a blue circle.

JAMES I

"Hmm. That can't be a coincidence" you said to me,
James.

Were you finally convinced?

You were visibly shaken by the betrayal
Of your machines; the inexplicable
Always put you on mute.

When you were ready, we spoke
Of solutions, steps, securing a legal phalanx

You finally believed me & I was
Ready for relief,
                    JUSTICE!
            VENGEANCE!!!

I hoarded more evidence. I was ecstatic.

"This could be a very long process"
You warned me, James

"We could spend the rest of our lives
Trying to prove this"

"I can think of no better way to spend
the rest of my days!" I urged,
fanning your dying flames,
James. "What could be

More important than solving this
Mystery, revealing the truth, setting the precedent?

What could be more paramount,
What could be tantamount to this mountainous range
Of violations &
      Validations,
Our voices located as echoes
In cyber sci-fi history?"

"I don't know," you said,
"I don't think I want to ride that train

Thru such mountainous terrain
I don't think you need validation
For these heinous violations.
Peace is more important,
Denial is tantamount to mute & drifting
Space debris
Come, float with me."

What To Make of Akathisia Thru a Blue Lens?

Maybe akathisia saved me
From devoting the next portion of my life
To pursuing a justice
That might've just
Been more ice,
Slipping around in my empty cup

But what is worse than akathisia?
Only a one-handed count of things.

Perhaps akathisia prevented me
From solving yet another mystery,
For without any confidence,
                    Or dopamine, or willing witnesses

The truth remains elusive

Were you there, Douglas,
Watching me shout at the angels, at all
My friends & relatives in the clouds?

Did you see me rolling on the bed
Trying to stop my shoulder blades
From beating like butterfly wings?

Trying to stand on knees
That turned to eels?

Where was your head, Douglas?
Why didn't you run for help?

JAMES II

Because akathisia is only better
Than being eaten by a shark,

I decided you were right, James.

I was ready to float away the remainder
Of my days… ·
Float as far as I could from any days in 2020
& on toward a future
Filled w/ space & quiet

So we siphoned ourselves
From the tubular state
That had been our home,

Away from its sock-like swelter &
Any thoughts of vengeance,
Any thoughts of Douglas,
Any thoughts of turning around,
Scrolling down that highway &
Finding no angel on the shoulder

Vin Whitman lived in Sarasota, FL for 78% of his life but left there when it became unrecognizable as the place he loved and inhabited with all his heart. He graduated from St Petersburg College in 1997 with an AS in Mortuary Science. All his artistic and literary mojo was earned on the sidelines.

Before attending college Vin was in a band called New Mind. Their single 'Closet Baby' was released by Cargo/Headhunter Records in 1992. If you Google it, you will find a lot of self-help content and closet organizers for nurseries. Sorry it was before the internet.

After attending college Vin worked in the funeral business for 3 years, then left to pursue more lighthearted endeavors. Such as fashion modeling, more music, and illustration. All of which he was a mild failure at.

Vin married his partner Tony in 1998, and they have stayed together despite the fact that Vin transitioned from female to male (starting 2014) and Tony only reads sci fi. Their life together has been one Tolkienesque adventure and Vin considers this relationship to be the best accomplishment of his life. So far.

Vin got involved in Sarasota's community radio (WSLR) in 2010 where he programmed several shows, including one with Tony as cohost. Vin and Tony departed Sarasota in 2021 and landed in Jasper, IN. Most days you can find them staring at their phones or playing with their rabbit on their front porch.

www.ingramcontent.com/pod-product-compliance
Lightning Source LLC
Chambersburg PA
CBHW020224090426
42734CB00008B/1207